TIGERS
HUNTERS OF ASIA

Norman Pearl

PowerKiDS press

New York

Published in 2009 by The Rosen Publishing Group, Inc.
29 East 21st Street, New York, NY 10010

First Edition

Editor: Amelie von Zumbusch
Book Design: Julio Gil
Photo Researcher: Jessica Gerweck

Photo Credits: Cover, pp. 5, 7, 9, 11, 13, 19, 21 Shutterstock.com; p. 15 © Anup Shah/Getty Images; p. 17 © Time & Life Pictures/Getty Images; back cover (top to bottom) Shutterstock.com, Shutterstock.com, © Kim Wolhuter/Getty Images, Shutterstock.com, © Stephen Frink/Getty Images, Shutterstock.com.

Library of Congress Cataloging-in-Publication Data

Pearl, Norman.
  Tigers : hunters of Asia / Norman Pearl. — 1st ed.
      p. cm. — (Powerful predators)
  Includes index.
  ISBN 978-1-4042-4507-5 (library binding)
  1. Tigers—Juvenile literature. I. Title.
  QL737.C23P377 2009
  599.756—dc22
                                                          2008006840

Manufactured in the United States of America

Contents

Much Bigger Than a House Cat

Do you know what the world's biggest cat is? It is the tiger. Tigers are members of the cat family, just as house cats are. Tigers are much bigger than house cats, though! Large **male** tigers weigh more than 600 pounds (272 kg). That is about as much as a large zebra weighs! A big male tiger can be up to 12 feet (4 m) long.

Besides being big, tigers are fast and strong. These large cats are great swimmers, too. Tigers have been known to swim across rivers that are almost 20 miles (32 km) wide!

As all cats are, tigers are predators, or hunters. Tigers are among the world's largest and strongest predators

That's Quite a Cat!

It is easy to recognize a tiger. Tigers are the only big cats with stripes. Most tigers have reddish-orange coats with dark stripes. There are also some white tigers with dark stripes. Each tiger's stripes are different.

Tigers have long claws to lock on to their **prey**. A tiger's claws are about 4 inches (10 cm) long. These big cats have powerful **jaws** as well. A tiger's jaws are also good for holding on to prey. Tigers have full sets of sharp teeth for tearing and chewing meat. Some tiger teeth are 3 inches (8 cm) long!

Tigers have lighter fur over their eyes, around their mouths, on their bellies, and on the insides of their legs.

Where Do You Find Tigers?

When many people think of tigers, they picture them living in Africa's **jungles**. However, tigers do not live in Africa at all! These big cats live only in Asia. Today, five types of tigers can be found throughout Asia. Some kinds of tigers live in very cold places, such as eastern Russia and northern China. Other tigers live in warmer places, such as southern India and Southeast Asia.

Wherever they live, tigers spend much of their time alone. Males and **females** come together to **mate**, though. About three months later, the female gives birth to two to three babies. Tiger babies are called cubs.

Amur tigers live in parts of Russia and China where it is often cold. They have extra thick fur to help them stay warm.

Tiger Babies

When a tiger cub is born, it is about as big as a house cat. A new tiger cub needs its mother for everything. Baby tigers are **blind** and do not open their eyes until they are two weeks old. At first, a cub lives on its mother's milk. Later its mother brings the cub meat she has caught.

Once a cub is about six months old, it starts going out with its mother. She teaches the cub to hunt. When it is between two and three years old, a young tiger leaves its mother to begin life on its own.

Young tigers are very interested in the world around them.
They like to climb, chase each other, and discover new things.

A Tiger's Territory

A grown tiger claims its own **territory** in which to live. A male tiger's territory often covers about 25 square miles (65 sq km), while a female's territory is generally between 8 and 10 square miles (21–26 sq km). Sometimes, a male tiger will share its territory with a female. However, a male tiger will never share its territory with another male.

Tigers mark their territories in different ways. Sometimes, they **scratch** the ground and trees. Tigers will also **urinate** on the ground, trees, bushes, and rocks. This marks their territories with their **scents**.

Every tiger's territory must have a stream, lake, pond, or river from which the tiger can drink.

Gifted Hunters

Tigers hunt for prey in their territories. They generally hunt after dark. These large cats are well prepared for hunting. They have good sight, great hearing, and an excellent sense of smell. These sharp senses help tigers find prey.

Tigers use both surprise and strength to get their prey. Sometimes, they will quietly trail an animal before they spring into action. Other times, a tiger will hide in high grass and wait for its prey to come along. Finding a good meal is not always easy. A tiger looking for food may have to travel 10 to 20 miles (16–32 km) in one night.

Tigers often creep up on their prey. These big cats can move very quietly and quickly.

What's for Supper?

All tigers are carnivores, or meat eaters. However, tigers in different parts of Asia catch different kinds of prey. Many tigers like deer and wild pigs. Sometimes, tigers will eat larger animals, such as baby elephants. However, tigers will eat whatever they can catch. A hungry tiger will even eat a frog, turtle, or bird. Though tigers eat other animals, no other animals eat tigers.

Tigers have been known to eat as much as 77 pounds (35 kg) of meat in one meal. If a tiger does not finish eating its prey, it will hide the prey to eat later.

This Bengal tiger from India's Kanha National Park is eating a buffalo that it caught.

Man-Eating Tigers

Tigers do not generally eat people. Yet some tigers, known as man-eaters, do prey on people. These tigers are often too old or too sick to **attack** healthy animals. Sadly, some tigers keep preying on people once they get a taste for them.

The place where tigers attack people most often is the Sundarbans, a **mangrove** forest in Asia. Tigers sometimes kill people gathering honey and wood there. Today, people in the Sundarbans wear masks on the backs of their heads to stay safe. Tigers do not like to attack from the front, and the masks make the tigers think the people are facing them.

Tigers are beautiful and interesting, but it is not safe to get too near them. They are predators with sharp claws and long teeth.

Tigers in Trouble

Though tigers have attacked people, people have attacked tigers much more often. Over the years, tigers have been hunted for sport. Their skins have been sold to make rugs and coats. Tiger body parts have brought high prices, too. In some parts of the world, these are thought to make you healthy. People have also taken away much of the tiger's **habitat**. People have cut down forests to make way for towns and farms.

Today, there are far fewer tigers than there were in the past. There may be fewer than 5,000 of these animals living in the wild.

Sumatran tigers are among the least common kinds of tigers.
There are only 400 to 500 Sumatran tigers living in the wild today.

Saving the Tiger

Sadly, the tiger is now an endangered species. That means that it might die out. However, people from many countries are working to save the tiger. New laws have been passed to keep these beautiful cats safe. In many places, it is now a crime to kill or hurt a tiger.

Tigers cannot live without a place to hunt and have their young. Luckily, land in India and other places is being set aside for the tiger. People around the world are working together to keep tigers safe so that we never lose these beautiful cats.

Glossary

attack (uh-TAK) To try to hurt someone or something.

blind (BLYND) Cannot use the sense of sight.

females (FEE-maylz) Women and girls.

habitat (HA-beh-tat) The kind of land where an animal or a plant naturally lives.

jaws (JAHZ) Bones in the top and bottom of the mouth.

jungles (JUNG-gulz) Land with lots of trees and plants, often in warm, wet places.

male (MAYL) Having to do with men and boys.

mangrove (MAN-grohv) A tree that grows in wetlands and along rivers.

mate (MAYT) To join together to make babies.

prey (PRAY) An animal that is hunted by another animal for food.

scents (SENTZ) Things that are sensed by the nose.

scratch (SKRACH) To rub or tear.

territory (TER-uh-tor-ee) Land or space that an animal guards for its use.

urinate (YER-ih-nayt) To pass watery wastes from the body.

23

Index

C

carnivores, 16

China, 8

claws, 6

H

habitat, 20

I

India, 8, 22

J

jaws, 6

L

laws, 22

M

meat, 6, 10, 16

milk, 10

P

prey, 6, 14, 16

R

Russia, 8

S

Southeast Asia, 8

sport, 20

stripes, 6

Sundarbans, 18

swimmers, 4

T

teeth, 6

Web Sites

Due to the changing nature of Internet links, PowerKids Press has developed an online list of Web sites related to the subject of this book. This site is updated regularly. Please use this link to access the list:

www.powerkidslinks.com/pred/tigers/